Carter Reads the Newspaper

The Story of Carter G. Woodson,
Founder of Black History Month

For Deborah Wiles and Jim Pearce

—D. H.

To the inspiring young men of Books 4 Buddies in Holland, Ohio (*books4buddies.com*).
Thank you for promoting literacy and building young leaders one book at a time.

—D. T.

Carter Reads the Newspaper

The Story of Dr. Carter G. Woodson, Founder of Black History Month

Written by **Deborah Hopkinson**

Illustrated by **Don Tate**

PEACHTREE
ATLANTA

Each February we celebrate Black History Month. It's a
time to honor heroes like Harriet Tubman, Rosa Parks,
and Martin Luther King Jr.

Harriet Tubman

A FEMALE CONDUCTOR OF THE UNDER-GROUND RAILROAD

At the late Woman's Rights Convention, at
Meoneleon Hall, Boston, the most interesting incident
was the appearance
man, Mrs
So
sc

Martin Luther King Jr.

Martin Luther King Jr., American Negro civil rights leader,
accepted the 1904 Nobel Peace
Prize today as
nition that

—A Negro woman was fined
$10 and costs in
to
na
tic
Rosa Parks, seamstress
do
se
signed by her Negro

Rosa Parks

But there's one hero we
sometimes forget.

Carter G. Woodson didn't help
people escape from slavery, start a
bus strike, or lead a movement of
millions. Yet without him, we might
not have Black History Month.

This is his story.

Carter was born on a small farm in Virginia in 1875, ten years after the end of the Civil War. Carter's parents, James Henry and Anne Eliza, were born into slavery, and Carter grew up hearing about their lives.

The stories they told weren't part of any history book. But Carter kept them in his heart.

James Henry had run away from his master to join the Union Army and fight for freedom.

Times were hard, though. After the war, James Henry worked on the railroad, saving enough to buy a few acres of worn-out land. Most years the crops brought in a hundred dollars or less.

James Henry Woodson

Anne Eliza was unbelievably brave. When she was a girl, her master decided to sell her mother. Anne Eliza asked him to sell her instead. That way her mother wouldn't have to leave her other five children. But no one offered enough money for Anne Eliza, so her master sold her mother and two little brothers instead. Anne Eliza didn't see them again until after the Civil War.

She never forgot the horror of standing on the auction block.

Anne Eliza Riddle Woodson

Carter's parents struggled to feed and clothe seven children. Especially in winter and early spring, food was scarce. Carter, the youngest, once said, "We would leave the table hungry to go to the woods and pluck the persimmons."

Many times he had to jump into bed early on Saturday nights so his mother could wash his only pants and shirt for church the next day.

Carter could only attend school four months each year. The rest of the time he was needed to work on the farm.

Learning didn't happen just at school. James Henry taught his children to stand up for themselves and take pride in who they were. He gave Carter the courage to look anyone in the eye and declare, "I am your equal."

And though Carter's father couldn't read or write, he believed in being an informed citizen. So he asked Carter to read the newspaper to him.

But newspapers weren't easy to come by. Sometimes Carter read from old ones that had been used to wrap up food or packages.

Reading the newspaper gave Carter his first glimpse of the wider world.

Carter longed to go to high school, but his family needed him to earn money.

When he was fifteen, he hired himself out to nearby farms, working long hours under the hot sun. He also drove a garbage wagon.

High school would have to wait.

Carter's older brother, Robert, found good paying work in the coal mines of West Virginia. Carter decided to join him there.

Mining was grueling work for a boy not yet seventeen. It was dangerous. Once, a piece of slate came crashing down on Carter's head.

He never forgot his time in the mines. Years later, Carter said, "I am a coal miner and I can take anything."

In this harsh place Carter met a man named Oliver Jones.

You'd have to look hard to find Oliver's name in a history book. But in that small mining camp in Fayette County, West Virginia, Oliver did something important: he changed one life, and that life changed many.

Oliver Jones

Like Carter's father, Oliver was a Civil War veteran who believed
in education.

As a soldier who had been at the Battle of Appomattox on the
final day of the Civil War, Oliver had fought for freedom and
equality. "He was still willing to do his part to further the cause,"
said Carter.

Each evening, after working in the mines, Oliver threw open the
doors of his little house to the other miners. He made his home a
reading room, filling it with books by African-American writers and
with newspapers from all over the country. He sold ice cream and
fruits, all at prices the men could afford.

At first, Carter just went for the food. But that changed. Carter said, "When Oliver Jones learned that I could read he soon engaged me to inform him and his friends as to what was in the daily newspapers."

Carter was happy to oblige. He liked reading the newspaper. Besides, he said later, "I always enjoyed nice things to eat."

Carter admired Oliver. "He was a well educated man, but he could neither read nor write," said Carter. "He learned through others."

Carter began to learn in the same way.

Carter had longed for school. Life at Oliver's tearoom turned out to be school of a different kind.

Whenever Oliver and the other miners had questions about something Carter read in the newspaper, it was Carter's job to research the answers.

If a Civil War veteran was in the news, Oliver wanted to know all about the man. "I had to look him up in the books, inform my friends as to what battles he had fought," said Carter.

If there was a question about economics, politics, or a new law, it was up to Carter to find out all about it in the newspaper and explain it to his friends.

Carter was inspired by Oliver and this circle of men committed to freedom, equality, and knowledge—men whose own life stories would never be in history books.

And so the seeds of Carter's own life work began to grow. "My interest in penetrating the past of my people was deepened."

Carter worked in the mines for three years. When he was twenty, Carter started at Frederick Douglass High School in Huntington, West Virginia. He finished in just two years. Carter went on to college and became a teacher. He continued to study and work, earning a master's degree when he was thirty-three.

Then, when Carter was thirty-seven, he earned a PhD in history from Harvard University, the second African American to do so. (W. E. B. Du Bois was the first.)

Carter was the first and only Black American whose parents had been slaves to receive a doctorate in history.

At Harvard, so the story goes, one of Carter's professors said that Black people had no history. Carter remembered his father's pride, his mother's courage, and Oliver's determination to learn. He remembered reading the newspaper.

Carter spoke up. "No people lacked a history," he said. The professor challenged Carter to prove him wrong.

For the rest of his life, Carter did just that.

In 1926, he established Negro History Week. (Later, it became Black History Month.) Carter chose the second week of February, to mark the birthdays of Frederick Douglass and Abraham Lincoln.

Today our entire nation celebrates Black History Month, and we honor Dr. Carter G. Woodson as the father of Black History. But in 1926, Carter was alone with his new idea. He had to blaze a trail.

Frederick Douglass

Abraham Lincoln

Sarah Breedlove

Rebecca Lee Crumpler

Peter Salem

Mary McLeod Bethune

George Washington Carver

Lewis Latimer

Ida B. Wells

Sojourner Truth

W.E.B. Du Bois

He had to spread the word at a time when there were no computers or internet or televisions. So Carter sent pamphlets about Negro History Week out to schools, colleges, churches, and women's clubs. And, of course, he sent notices to newspapers.

The boy who began by reading the newspaper to others
transformed the way people thought about history. He fought for
a history based on truth—a history that includes all people.

Carter G. Woodson didn't just study history. He changed it.

And we can too.

Learn More About Carter G. Woodson

Internet Resources

Association for the Study of African American Life and History (ASALH)
www.asalh.org

Carter G. Woodson Home, National Park Service
www.nps.gov/cawo/index.htm

Encyclopedia Virginia
www.encyclopediavirginia.org/Woodson_Carter_G_1875-1950

Bibliography

Dagbovie, Pero Gaglo. *Carter G. Woodson in Washington, D.C.: The Father of Black History*. Charleston, SC: History Press, 2014.

The Early Black History Movement, Carter G. Woodson, and Lorenzo Johnston Greene. Chicago: University of Illinois Press, 2007.

Goggin, Jacqueline. *Carter G. Woodson: A Life in Black History*. Baton Rouge: Louisiana State University Press, 1993.

*Haskins, Jim and Kathleen Benson. *Carter G. Woodson: The Man who Put "Black" in American History*. Brookfield, CT: Millbrook Press, 2000.

*McKissack, Patricia and Frederick McKissack. *Carter G. Woodson: The Father of Black History*. Berkeley Heights, N.J.: Enslow Publishers, Inc., 2002, 1991.

*McKissack, Pat. *Carter G. Woodson: Black History Pioneer*. Berkeley Heights, N.J.: Enslow Publishers, Inc., 2013.

Scally, Sister Anthony. *Carter G. Woodson: A Bio-Bibliography*. Westport, CN: Greenwood Press, 1985.

Woodson, Carter G. "My Recollections of Veterans of the Civil War." *Negro History Bulletin*, VII, February 1944. pages 103–104, 115–118.

For young readers

Author's Note

"The teaching of the whole truth will help us in the direction of a real democracy."

—Carter G. Woodson, 1944

Dr. Carter G. Woodson worked throughout his life to fight against the idea that African Americans had no history. He conducted groundbreaking research, and built a movement to honor and recognize African-American contributions to history that is still alive and vibrant. The organization he founded in 1915 thrives today as ASALH, the Association for the Study of African American Life and History. In 1976, his home and office headquarters in Washington, DC, was designated a National Historic Landmark.

Dr. Woodson reminded us that ordinary people belong in history. He himself was inspired by listening to his parents and Civil War veterans like Oliver Jones. Dr. Woodson also understood the importance of a free press, and the need for more books about African Americans. "Ask repeatedly for such books," he wrote in 1940. "Show that there is a demand for them." In his honor, in 1974, the National Council of the Social Studies established the Carter G. Woodson Book Award to recognize the most distinguished social science books appropriate for young readers that depict ethnicity in the United States.

Dr. Woodson also believed in "raising high the standard of the truth." He said, "Upon this principle and on this only can a real democracy be built."

As I researched Dr. Woodson, I found myself wishing he had left us more personal stories about his own fascinating life. Perhaps he was simply too busy working to bring African-American history to everyone in America. We are all still learning from him.

—Deborah Hopkinson

Illustrator's Note

I grew up in Des Moines, Iowa, in the 1960s and 70s—not exactly a place one thinks of as a bastion of Black cultural awareness. But believe it or not, there was a small but lively African-American community of scholars, entrepreneurs, artists, poets, writers, activists, and more.

I didn't learn much about my Black history in grade school—although I do remember an occasional bulletin board decorated with figures like Harriet Tubman and George Washington Carver. But there weren't any meaningful discussions or books about these people.

What I learned about Black history was gleaned from programs offered through the Center for Study and Application of Black Theology (or The Black Theology Center, as we called it), at the corner of Eleventh Street and Forest Avenue, in the heart of the Black community.

The Center's mission was to help foster an awareness of the need for Black unity, pride, and self-identity. We learned about historical figures such as Marcus Garvey, Mary McLeod Bethune, Charles Drew, Booker T. Washington, and other Black history figures who never showed up on those bulletin boards at school.

In addition to Black history, we also learned some Swahili, a language spoken in East Africa, including words like *Umoja* (unity); *Kujichagulia* (self-determination), and *Ujima* (collective work and responsibility). We celebrated Kwanzaa, an African-American holiday observed during the week following Christmas, and we learned about the meaning of the colors of the Black national flag: red for the blood of Black people; black for Black people; green for land and power.

It was a warm, friendly environment, where Black intellectuals, dressed in colorful dashikis, wore large, perfectly sculpted naturals (afros), and discussed current events, sports, and politics over games of chess. I don't know this for sure, but I would bet the Center was inspired by the work of Carter G. Woodson.

—Don Tate

The following Black leaders are pictured throughout the book:

Muhammad Ali (1942–2016) athlete and civil rights activist

Queen Amina (c. 1533–1610) Hausa warrior queen of Zazzau (now part of Nigeria)

Marian Anderson (1897–1993) singer and civil rights activist

Maya Angelou (1928–2014) poet, author, and civil rights activist

Hannibal Barca (247–182 BC) general in the Carthage military (now Tunisia)

Mary McLeod Bethune (1875–1955) educator and civil rights activist

Sarah Breedlove (1867–1919) entrepreneur, philanthropist, and activist, also known as Madam C. J. Walker

George Washington Carver (c. 1860–1943) botanist and inventor

Shirley Chisholm (1924–2005) first African-American congresswoman

Joseph Cinqué (c. 1814–c. 1879) leader of the African revolt on the slave ship Amistad

Rebecca Lee Crumpler (1831–1895) physician and author

Frederick Douglass (c. 1818–1895) abolitionist and author

Charles Drew (1904–1950) surgeon; creator of early blood banks

W. E. B. Du Bois (1868–1963) historian, author, and civil rights activist

Duke Ellington (1899–1974) composer, musician, and bandleader

Marcus Garvey (1887–1940) leader of the Pan-Africanism movement

Frances Harper (1825–1911) abolitionist, suffragist, and author

Zora Neale Hurston (1891–1960) author and anthropologist

Mae Jemison (1956–) engineer, physician, and astronaut; the first African-American woman in space

Katherine Johnson (1918–) mathematician whose work led to the first successful US space flight

Colin Kaepernick (1987–) athlete and civil rights activist

Coretta Scott King (1927–2006) author and civil rights activist

Martin Luther King Jr. (1929–1968) minister, author, and civil rights activist

Lewis Latimer (1848–1928) engineer and inventor

Edmonia Lewis (1844–1907) first African-American and Native American female sculptor to achieve international recognition

Malcolm X (1925–1965) religious leader and civil rights activist

Elijah McCoy (1844–1929) inventor and engineer

Mansa Musa (c. 1280—c. 1337) sultan of the Mali Empire (now Southern Mauritania and Mali)

Nzinga of Ndongo (c. 1583–1663) queen of the Ndongo and Matamba Kingdoms of the Mbundu people (now Angola)

Barack Obama (1961–) 44th President of the United States

Michelle Obama (1964–) lawyer, author, and former First Lady of the United States

Jesse Owens (1913–1980) four-time Olympic gold medalist in track and field

Rosa Parks (1913–2005) civil rights activist and leader of the Montgomery Bus Boycott

Peter Salem (1750–1816) soldier in the American Revolution

Dred Scott (c. 1799–1858) enslaved man who unsuccessfully sued for his freedom and that of his family

Taharqa (reign 690–664 BC) Egyptian pharaoh

Sojourner Truth (c. 1797–1883) abolitionist and suffragist

Harriet Tubman (c. 1820–1913) abolitionist who rescued numerous enslaved people

Nat Turner (1800–1831) leader of a rebellion of slaves and free Blacks

Booker T. Washington (1856–1915) educator and author

Ida B. Wells (1862–1931) journalist and civil rights activist

Phillis Wheatley (1753–1784) first published Black female poet

Richard Wright (1908–1960) journalist and author

Carter Godwin Woodson's Life and Accomplishments

1875   Born in New Canton, Virginia, on December 19.

1892   Moves to West Virginia to work as a coal miner at the age of seventeen.

1895   Enters high school, which he completes in two years.

1897   Enters Berea College in Kentucky, receiving a bachelor's degree in 1903.

1903   Travels to the Philippines to teach.

1908   Earns a master's degree from the University of Chicago.

1912   Becomes second African American (after W. E. B. Du Bois) to receive a PhD from Harvard University, and the first child of enslaved parents to earn a doctorate in history.

1915   Publishes *The Education of the Negro Prior to 1861*, his first book, and founds the Association for the Study of Negro Life and History in Washington, DC, where he was teaching high school. Today known as Association for the Study of African American Life and History (ASALH), it is the oldest organization dedicated to the study and promotion of Black history.

1916   Publishes first issue of *The Journal of Negro History*.

1926   Founds Negro History Week, to be observed in February, in honor of the birthdays of Frederick Douglass and Abraham Lincoln.

1930s   Continues to publish and is also active in civil rights, including the National Association for the
–1940s Advancement of Colored People's anti-lynching efforts.

1950   Dies in Washington, DC, on April 3 at the age of seventy-four.

Quotations in the text are from the following sources:

9   "We would leave the table…"
      Woodson, C. "And the Negro Loses His Soul," *Chicago Defender*, June 25, 1932.
      Quoted in *Carter G. Woodson in Washington, D.C.* by Pero Gaglo Dagbovie, page 34.

10   "I am your equal…"
      Dagbovie, page 33.

14   "I am a coal miner…"
      Dagbovie, page 34.

17   "He was still willing…"
      Woodson, C. "My Recollections of Veterans of the Civil War." *Negro History Bulletin*, VII, February 1944,
      page 116.

18   All quotations from "My Recollections of Veterans of the Civil War."

20   "I had to look him up…"
      "My Recollections of Veterans of the Civil War."

21   "My interest in penetrating…"
      "My Recollections of Veterans of the Civil War."

25   "No people lacked a history…"
      Dagbovie, page 40.

Published by
PEACHTREE PUBLISHING COMPANY INC.
1700 Chattahoochee Avenue
Atlanta, Georgia 30318-2112
PeachtreeBooks.com

First trade paperback edition published in 2021

Edited by Kathy Landwehr
Design and composition by Nicola Simmonds Carmack

The illustrations were created using mixed media.

Printed in April 2023 by Toppan Leefung Printing Limited in China
10 9 8 7 6 (hardcover)
10 9 8 7 6 5 4 3 (paperback)

HC ISBN: 978-1-56145-934-6
PB ISBN: 978-1-68263-332-8

Library of Congress Cataloging-in-Publication Data

Names: Hopkinson, Deborah, author. | Tate, Don, illustrator.
Title: Carter reads the newspaper / written by Deborah Hopkinson ; illustrated by Don Tate.
Description: Atlanta, Georgia : Peachtree Publishers, [2019]
Identifiers: LCCN 2018002739 | ISBN 9781561459346
Subjects: LCSH: Woodson, Carter Godwin, 1875-1950—Juvenile literature. | Woodson, Carter Godwin, 1875-1950—Books and reading—Juvenile literature. | African American historians—Biography—Juvenile literature | Historians—United States—Juvenile literature.
Classification: LCC E175.5.W65 H67 2019 | DDC 973/.0496073007202 [B] —dc23 LC record available at *https://lccn.loc.gov/2018002739*